D0834679

LIVING
WITH
CANCER

a story of hope, courage, and new life...
born out of darkness

barbara k. linton

WESTBOW
P R E S S®
A DIVISION OF THOMAS NELSON
& ZONDERVAN

Scripture taken from the King James Version of the Bible.

Scripture taken from the New King James Version. Copyright 1979, 1980,
1982 by Thomas Nelson, inc. Used by permission. All rights reserved.

WestBow Press books may be ordered through booksellers or by contacting:

WestBow Press
A Division of Thomas Nelson & Zondervan
1663 Liberty Drive
Bloomington, IN 47403
www.westbowpress.com
1 (866) 928-1240

ISBN: 978-1-5127-0171-5 (sc)
ISBN: 978-1-5127-0172-2 (e)

Print information available on the last page.

WestBow Press rev. date: 08/09/2016

This is a true story—not one that happened to someone else, but the story of what actually happened in my own life. What you will read is a step-by-step journey of the ups and downs, challenges and triumphs of a life with cancer.

In these pages, you will see how each day brought various struggles, and how God was faithful to meet each need, time and time again. I have put my journey on paper to emphasize this point,—to share words of encouragement with others who find themselves on the path that I have traveled. To let you know that you do not have to walk this difficult journey alone. God loves you and is ready and able to give you strength to walk triumphantly through whatever life brings your way.

As you read, *Living with Cancer*, I pray these personal experiences of God's faithfulness in times of difficulty and pain, along with Scriptures of hope and encouragement, will draw you closer to the Lord. May your life be blessed, strengthened, and transformed as mine has through this journey with cancer.

Contents

✠ The Journey Begins—"Fear Not"

It was the spring of 2008 and time for my annual check-up. I was forty-six years old and unconcerned about anything being wrong physically. After all, I was young and felt fine! I just wanted to get this appointment behind me and not have to think about it again for another year.

But this year's check-up would be different from any I had had in previous years. This year, after my appointment, I received a phone call from the doctor's office asking me to return for some additional tests. This turned in to a *month* of medical procedures, tests, and a biopsy, none of which I had ever experienced before.

I didn't know it at the time, but my life was about to take a wide turn down a path I had never traveled before. Questions flooded my mind about what was wrong in my body and what was ahead. Still, my heart and soul were at peace. How could this be? Suddenly, my world was changing. And I had *peace?*

I had believed in God for many years and had striven to live my life according to the Scriptures. Was my faith in God going to be sufficient to carry me through what was ahead? This was real life. This was where "the rubber met the road!"

As I clung to God in prayer each day and searched the Scriptures for answers as to what was happening in my life, the Lord gently spoke to my heart over and over again, comforting me with His words, "Fear not."

> "Fear not: for I have redeemed thee, I have called thee by thy name; thou art mine. When thou passest through the waters, I will be with thee; and through the rivers, they shall not overflow thee: when thou walkest through the fire, thou shalt not be burned; neither shall the flame kindle upon thee" (Isaiah 43:1b-2 KJV).

> "Fear not: for I am with thee" (Isaiah 43:5a).

> "Thus saith the LORD, which maketh a way in the sea, and a path in the mighty waters; Remember ye not the former things, neither consider the things of old. Behold, I will do a new thing; now it shall spring forth; shall ye not know it? I will even make a way in the wilderness, and rivers in the desert" (Isaiah 43:16, 18-19).

> "Thou art my servant; I have chosen thee, and not cast thee away. Fear thou not, for I am with thee: be not dismayed; for I am thy God: I will strengthen thee; yea, I will help thee; yea, I will uphold thee with the right hand of my righteousness" (Isaiah 41:9b-10).

Are *you* starting out on a new journey in life? You don't have to be afraid. Turn to the Lord right now in prayer, ask Him to take away your fear, to fill you with His perfect peace, and to guide and protect you in the days ahead.

Thank you, God, for Your promises that bring comfort and peace to my soul! Help me to "fear not", as I trust You completely with my life. Thank you, Lord, that You have a master plan and whatever these tests reveal to me is no surprise to You. Continue to strengthen my faith and trust in You, Lord.

"I sought the Lord, and he heard me, and delivered me from all my fears" (Psalm 34:4).

✝ It's the Lord's Battle

When things aren't going well and trials and tribulations seem to be on every hand, do you want to run and hide? When you are attacked from every direction, do you lose heart and quit?

Remember, God is faithful, and He never changes, even when our circumstances do. In our darkest hours, we must run *to* God, not *away* from Him!

> "And the people fled from the Philistines. But he stood in the midst of the ground, and defended it, and slew the Philistines: and the Lord wrought a great victory" (II Samuel 23:11b–12).

Lord, help me to stand firm in You and to remember this is Your battle, not mine. May I see You bring a great victory in and through my life, that Your name may be praised among the people.

> "Be strong and of a good courage, fear not, nor be afraid of them: for the LORD thy God, he it is that doth

go with thee; he will not fail thee, nor forsake thee" (Deuteronomy 31:6).

"Jesus Christ is the same yesterday and today and forever" (Hebrews 13:8).

✝ You're Not Alone

The day of the MRI was another new experience and another day of faith through the unknown. The technician explained how the test would be done, positioned me, and then left the room. As I lay on the table, the Lord brought Psalm 23 to my mind. The words kept going over and over in my mind as the test was being done, and I knew I wasn't alone. God was with me.

At this moment, do you feel alone? Do you sense clouds all around you with no sunshine in sight? Turn to Jesus, the Good Shepherd, and let Him lead you through the dark times of your life and into His marvelous light.

> "The Lord is my shepherd; I shall not want. He maketh me to lie down in green pastures: he leadeth me beside the still waters. He restoreth my soul: he leadeth me in the paths of righteousness for his name's sake. Yea, though I walk through the valley of the shadow of death, I will fear no evil: for thou art with me; thy rod and thy staff they comfort me" (Psalm 23:1–4).

"The LORD is my light and my salvation; whom shall I fear? The LORD is the strength of my life; of whom shall I be afraid?" (Psalm 27:1).

Thank you, God, that no matter what I face, I'm not alone! You are right here with me, holding my hand and filling me with Your perfect peace and rest.

✝ Trusting God

The Friday before Mother's Day, I was back at the doctor's office for another procedure. To my surprise, the medical procedure lead to another discovery and subsequent biopsy. The doctor said the preliminary test results looked "suspicious," and the biopsy would be sent to the lab for further analysis. It would be Monday before I would have an answer as to what was going on in my body.

As I waited for the final test results, I searched for direction from the Lord and encouragement for my soul as I went to the Lifeway Christian Book Store on Saturday. As I entered the store, a woman was greeting customers and handing out bookmarks. When I looked at the bookmark, I saw a message that spoke directly to my heart:

> "And thine ears shall hear a word behind thee, saying: This is the way, walk ye in it, when ye turn to the right hand, and when ye turn to the left" (Isaiah 30:21).

God's peace immediately flooded my soul as I was once again reminded of His presence and guiding hand in my life.

Thank you, God, for the power in Your words which still guide and direct us today. Help me, as I wait for the final test results, to listen to Your words for direction in my life. Strengthen my trust in You, Lord, and may I follow You wherever this path may lead.

"Thy word is a lamp unto my feet and a light unto my path" (Psalm 119:105).

"Trust in the LORD with all thine heart; and lean not unto thine own understanding. In all thy ways acknowledge him and he shall direct thy paths" (Proverbs 3:5-6).

✝ "It Is Malignant"

The doctor's office had become all too familiar in recent weeks. As I walked in on the Monday after Mother's Day, I knew something was going on in my body, but what? Were all the tests finally over? Would I finally have a diagnosis?

The doctor came in and shared the test results with me. It was then that I heard words I never thought I would hear: "It is malignant."

As I began mentally processing this news, questions began flooding my mind. My whole life was about to change. I was starting down a road I'd never traveled before, about to encounter people I'd never met, in places I'd never been. I had *cancer*. *What does the future hold for me?* I wondered.

Yet, deep in my soul, I felt a perfect peace that could only come from God at such a time as this. I knew this diagnosis was no surprise to Him. And, regardless of the storms that were brewing in my life, God still had the power to calm the raging seas.

"And there arose a great storm of wind, and the waves beat into the ship, so that it was now full. And he was in the hinder part of the ship, asleep on a pillow: and they awake him, and say unto him, Master, carest thou not that we perish? And he arose, and rebuked the wind, and said unto the sea, Peace, be still. And the wind ceased, and there was a great calm" (Mark 4:37-39).

"God is our refuge and strength, a very present help in trouble" (Psalm 46:1).

"Beloved, think it not strange concerning the fiery trial which is to try you, as though some strange thing happened unto you: but rejoice, inasmuch as ye are partakers of Christ's sufferings; that, when his glory shall be revealed, ye may be glad also with exceeding joy" (1 Peter 4:12–13).

Oh, God, this is a fiery trial! Please protect me, Lord, in this storm that is brewing! I know You are the Great Physician with the power to heal my body, and I know You are more powerful than any cancer could ever be! Please work in my life, Lord, according to Your will and give me strength physically, mentally, and spiritually to face what is ahead. My life is in Your hands.

✝ When You Don't Understand, Trust His Heart

As I contemplated the last few weeks of my life, I praised the Lord for leading the medical staff to find the cancer. The malignancy did not show up on the original test—another area of concern did! It wasn't until I went back to have this other concern treated that the doctor found the cancer.

What if nothing had shown up during the annual check-up? I wondered. *What if the results had stated that everything was fine? What if the cancer had not been detected until the next year's physical exam?* I would be in a much different state than I was thanks to the "accidental" discovery!

Even in the midst of this devastating news that no one ever wants to hear, I could see the Lord's hand at work in my life, and I praised Him for His love, guidance, and care.

"For I know the thoughts that I think toward you, says the LORD, thoughts of peace and not of evil, to give you a future and a hope" (Jeremiah 29:11 NKJV).

"As for God, his way is perfect: the word of the LORD is tried: he is a buckler to all those that trust in him" (Psalm 18:30).

Dear God, I don't understand why this is happening to me, but I can see Your guiding hand at work in my life. Strengthen my faith and trust in You, God, and continue to led me through this storm. My life is in Your hands, Lord.

Broken and Surrendered

After receiving the diagnosis, I wondered how my life would change. I had never had any health issues before, and everything I had been going through for the past few weeks had been one new experience after another. Now I had cancer and I didn't know what the future held.

One thing, however, I did know: Being the private person that I was, I knew I wasn't going to tell anyone I had cancer. My plan was to have outpatient surgery on a Friday, recover over the weekend, and go back to work the next week—all without telling a soul what I was going through. After all, what was going on in my body was personal and not something I wanted to share with others.

God, however, had another plan.

When I got home from the doctor's office, I headed straight for the living room, where I prayed and read the Scriptures each day. With tears running down my face and my heart heavy with an overwhelming burden, I sank onto my knees and prayed, asking God to let this cup pass from me. I *yearned* to not have cancer. I couldn't bear the thought of enduring the coming days. *How can this be happening to me?* I asked myself and God.

Then through the tears and with a broken heart I prayed, *Not my will, but Thine be done.* I felt like Jesus praying in the Garden of Gethsemane; I didn't know what was before me, but I trusted the Lord and His will for my life. I surrendered *all.*

It was then that the Lord reminded me that we do not have to carry our burdens alone—He is with us and will be with us *always,* sometimes right beside us, and sometimes carrying us when the road gets long and weary and no end is in sight. We just have to turn to Him and let Him carry us all the way.

> "Yea, though I walk through the valley of the shadow of death, I will fear no evil: for thou art with me; thy rod and thy staff they comfort me" (Psalm 23:4).

Won't you surrender your life to the Lord? He loves you and will walk with you every moment of your life if you will only ask Him.

Dear Jesus, I need You in my life. This [name your burden] is too much for me to carry alone. Please come into my heart and walk with me every step of the way. I surrender my life to You, Lord.

✝ First Oncology Visit— I'm Slipping, Lord!

My first visit to the oncology office was depressing! I didn't feel like I had cancer, so I kept myself mentally in a different category from those who did. After all, I was young, I didn't feel sick, and I had never been in the hospital except when my two sons were born.

Now I was in the same boat as the other people in the oncology office—all of us had been touched in some way by cancer! My faith was shaken.

Do you ever feel like you are slipping deeper and deeper into despair and can find no way out? In those times, remember that Jesus is our Rock, and even when the storms of life beat down upon us and we feel like we are on sinking sand, God is the solid Rock that cannot be moved. He will not let you sink. He's reaching out His hand to you and will draw you unto Himself. Just take His hand and let Him lead you to a safe harbor beside Him.

"He brought me up also out of an horrible pit, out of the miry clay, and set my feet upon a rock, and established my goings" (Psalm 40:2).

I'm slipping, Lord! Please get my feet out of the miry clay and put them back on the Solid Rock.

✤ Decisions to Make

As I met with the surgeon for the first time, I learned more about my condition. Prior to the appointment, I had thought I could simply have outpatient surgery and then be back to work almost immediately. However, when I met with the doctor, she explained the seriousness of my condition. Although outpatient surgery was an option, to my surprise, she also shared information about a more extensive and aggressive type of surgery. Now I had a decision to make regarding my treatment process in my fight against cancer.

What about you? Do you have some decisions to make? Are you researching information, getting second opinions, and contemplating the best direction for your life and health?

Remember, God understands all things and knows what to do. After all, He is the Creator and Sustainer of life! *Ask Him* to give you wisdom and knowledge regarding the path you should take, and then *trust Him* to walk with you down that path, rain or shine, smooth or rough, short or long, until you meet Him face to face one day in heaven.

"Has thou not known? Has thou not heard, that the everlasting God, the Lord, the Creator of the ends of the earth, fainteth not, neither is weary? There is no searching of his understanding. He giveth power to the faint; and to them that have no might he increaseth strength. Even the youths shall faint and be weary, and the young men shall utterly fall: But they that wait upon the Lord shall renew their strength; they shall mount up with wings as eagles; they shall run, and not be weary; and they shall walk, and not faint" (Isaiah 40:28–31).

"Trust in the Lord with all thine heart, and lean not unto thine own understanding. In all thy ways acknowledge him, and he shall direct thy paths" (Proverbs 3:5–6).

"Cause me to hear thy loving kindness in the morning; for in thee do I trust: cause me to know the way wherein I should walk, for I lift up my soul unto thee" (Psalm 143:8).

Dear God, show me the path that I should take. Guide me, Lord, and help me make the right decision regarding surgery!

☩ God Has a Plan for Our Lives

Although the Lord had personally given me peace about my condition, I had not told anyone, other than my husband, that I had cancer. I had never been one to share the personal details of my life with others, and this time was not any different. I didn't want to tell people what I was going through, especially when I didn't even know all that I was dealing with myself.

But God had a plan, and as I was out walking and praying in my neighborhood one evening, the Lord gently spoke to my heart and said, *I can't use this if you don't tell them.*

At that moment I realized God wanted to use the cancer in my life for His glory! I realized that having cancer at this exact time in my life was no accident. God did have a plan, and this was the path He had for me!

As I pondered these thoughts, my heart rejoiced, because again I was reminded that God was with me, that He loved me, and that He was leading my life. I then realized that I couldn't just tell people I was having surgery; I also had to tell them I had cancer. I couldn't hide what God was trying to do through me.

This mission was very difficult, but I trusted the Lord; I knew I had to be obedient to Him so that He could work through me.

Are you having a difficult time sharing with others what is happening in your life? Are you afraid to tell them that you have cancer? Trust in the Lord—He *does* have a plan for your life!

> "For I know the thoughts that I think toward you, says the LORD, thoughts of peace and not of evil, to give you a future and a hope" (Jeremiah 29:11).

Dear Jesus, I know You have a plan for me. Please help me to trust You completely. Give me the ability to share with others what is happening in my life and to see You work through this cancer for Your glory.

✝ The Night before Surgery

On the night before surgery, I received a phone call from Kim, whom I had met many years earlier. We had reconnected only briefly the previous year as she taught my son voice lessons at college.

As we talked, Kim shared with me how she had also just been diagnosed with cancer and would undergo surgery and follow-up treatments. Unaware of what I was going through at the time, she told me how she had felt the Lord directing her to call me that evening!

We connected instantly, and I was able, for the first time, to share with someone other than my immediate family what was happening in my life. The Lord was beginning to change me, gradually, from the private person that I was into the person He wanted me to be.

As I spoke with Kim, God used her as such an encouragement to me! God knew what I needed the night before surgery, and He reminded me that He was there, walking beside me, meeting my needs.

Jesus is the friend that is closer than a brother. You can talk with Him in prayer at any time and share with Him what is happening in your life. He listens and He cares about you!

> "Two are better than one, because they have a good reward for their labor. For if they fall, the one will lift up his fellow" (Ecclesiastes 4:9–10).

> "There is a friend who sticks closer than a brother" (Proverbs 18:24).

Thank you, God, for people you bring into our lives, just when we most need them! Thank you for the way You are working in my life, and for the peace that comes in knowing You have a purpose for this journey with cancer. Continue to strengthen my faith in You, God, as I continue on this untrodden path.

✝ Your Life Is a Shining Light to Others

For a long time, I had wanted to tell people about my faith in God and His love for them, but I was scared to do so. Maybe I was scared of rejection or of not having the right words to say. Either way, I had the *desire* to share my faith, but not the *confidence*.

Now the Lord was showing me that He wanted to use *me* to tell others about Him. He was teaching me, through the Scriptures, that I had a mouth and that He wanted me to use it to tell others about His love for them.

The physicians had been working on my physical body, but God had been working on my heart and spirit. I felt inadequate, but I trusted the Lord to guide me; with His power, I could now share with others, at least one-on-one, what God had been doing in my life. This change from keeping my personal life private to now sharing it with others was dramatic for me.

What is God doing in your life? Who does God want you to talk to about Him? Our lives are to be shining lights to others. Are you hiding your light under a bushel, or are you putting it on a candlestick for all to see?

> "Ye are the light of the world. A city that is set on a hill cannot be hid. Neither do men light a candle and put it under a bushel, but on a candlestick; and it giveth light unto all that are in the house. Let your light so shine before men, that they may see your good works, and glorify your Father which is in heaven" (Matthew 5:14-16).

> "But ye shall be witnesses unto me both in Jerusalem, and in all Judea, and in Samaria, and unto the uttermost part of the earth" (Acts 1:8).

> "Follow me, and I will make you fishers of men" (Matthew 4:19).

Thank you, God, for the work You are doing in my life. Please help me to be a shining light for You.

✠ Disappointments

My body was healing slowly from the surgery, and I was looking forward to putting all this behind me and getting my life back to normal. Then came the news of the pathology report from the surgery. The results were not as positive as I had thought they would be; and, in fact, the report showed more issues of concern which needed to be handled.

At this point, the doctor recommended follow-up treatments—not just radiation, but chemotherapy as well! *How could this be?* I wondered. *If there was ever one thing in my life I didn't want to go through, it was chemotherapy treatments!*

It was at this moment that I realized this journey with cancer wasn't over yet—in fact, it was just beginning. The oncologist's recommended course of treatment was strong, and I would lose my hair, become weak and nauseated. At first, I joked with the doctor, stating that my husband and my boys were the ones in the family who wore the hats, *not me*! Then reality began to set in and the tears began to flow. Chemotherapy treatments?!

As my husband and I arrived back home from the oncology office, I again knelt in the living room with a broken heart and prayed, seeking the Lord's strength for what was ahead. *Chemotherapy?* I questioned. *How am I ever going to be able to endure this kind of treatment?*

As I prayed and sought the Lord's guidance and peace in my life, the Holy Spirit reminded me again of these verses:

> "Fear not: for I have redeemed thee, I have called thee by thy name; thou art mine. When thou passest through the waters, I will be with thee; and through the rivers, they shall not overflow thee: when thou walkest through the fire, thou shalt not be burned; neither shall the flame kindle upon thee" (Isaiah 43:1b-2).

> "Fear not: for I am with thee" (Isaiah 43:5a).

> "Thus saith the LORD, which maketh a way in the sea, and a path in the mighty waters; Remember ye not the former things, neither consider the things of old. Behold, I will do a new thing; now it shall spring forth; shall ye not know it? I will even make a way in the wilderness, and rivers in the desert" (Isaiah 43:16, 18-19).

> "As I was with Moses, so I will be with thee: I will not fail thee, nor forsake thee. Be strong and of a good courage" (Joshua 1:5b-6a).

"Have not I commanded thee? Be strong and of a good courage; be not afraid, neither be thou dismayed: for the LORD thy God is with thee whithersoever thou goest" (Joshua 1:9).

As I continued to seek the Lord, He gently spoke to my heart and said, *You can't relate to others with cancer without going through this (chemotherapy and radiation). I want to use this for My glory.* I was reminded yet again that God wanted to use the cancer in my life, and now I must go through the treatment process as well, in order to be able to relate to others who were on the same path.

The Lord also spoke to my heart about not going back to being the same person I was before the cancer. God had been working in my life, forming me into a vessel He could use in a new way. I didn't know what this "new way" meant—where the Lord would lead me from this point—but my faith and trust were in Him, and I knew I would follow wherever He led.

Are you dealing with disappointments in your journey with cancer? Do you feel overwhelmed and devastated about the news of the challenging treatments that lie ahead? Then turn to Jesus in prayer right now. He knows your pain, anxiety, and fears, and He has His arms open wide, ready to receive you into His loving care. Trust Him completely with your life, rest in His arms, and let Him walk with you through the days ahead, step by step, all the way.

Dear Jesus, please hear my cry. I need You, Lord! These challenges are too much for me to face alone. Please take away my fear and give me peace and strength to face what lies ahead.

✝ Waiting and Resting

Several weeks after the surgery, I found myself in a waiting period—waiting for my body to heal, waiting on a second opinion regarding follow-up treatment, waiting to see where this journey would lead me next. *What does the Lord have for me from here?*

As I pondered these questions, my sister reminded me of this verse:

"Be still, and know that I am God" (Psalm 46:10a).

Are you in a time of waiting? Then remember these verses.

"Wait on the LORD: be of good courage, and he shall strengthen thine heart: wait, I say, on the Lord" (Psalm 27:14).

"But they that wait upon the LORD shall renew their strength; they shall mount up with wings as eagles;

they shall run, and not be weary; and they shall walk, and not faint" (Isaiah 40:31).

Dear Lord, thank you for bringing me safely through the surgery. Continue to heal my body and strengthen me, Lord, as I wait and rest in You.

✟ Compassion and Care

are is such a small word, but it means so much. As I went from one medical office to another, I personally experienced what it means to be cared for; these people did not know me, yet they showed genuine care to me in every way. They smiled at me, offered to help me, answered questions, explained my next steps, and so on. On two different occasions, the surgeon even gave me her cell-phone number in case my husband or I had any questions or needed her help!

God wants each of us to be caring and compassionate people. We encounter people each day that the Lord brings across our path. We may not know them, their backgrounds, their hurts or disappointments in life, but we need to show them that Jesus cares for them and that we care, too.

Luke 10:33-34 says,

> "But a certain Samaritan, as he journeyed, came where he was: and when he saw him, he had compassion on

31

him. And went to him, and bound up his wounds, pouring in oil and wine, and set him on his own beast, and brought him to an inn, and took care of him."

Jesus had compassion for the people around Him, which moved Him to minister to their needs. What are *you* doing to minister to others in need?

"And Jesus, when he came out, saw much people, and was moved with compassion toward them, because they were as sheep not having a shepherd" (Mark 6:34).

Lord, help me to have compassion for others. Teach me to reach out to them and show them Your love and genuine care for their souls and their lives.

✝ Walking through the Fires of Life

We read in the Scriptures in Daniel chapter 3 about Shadrach, Meshach, and Abednego being cast into the fiery furnace. They were faithfully serving God, and trouble came into their lives. In fact, the king had them thrown into the furnace *because* they obeyed God!

None of us are immune to trials and tribulations in life. At some point, all of us will encounter difficulties as we are cast into various "fires"--even when we are doing right and serving God! How do you respond in these situations? Do you draw closer to the Lord for protection and strength during the "fire", or do you turn your back and walk away from God?

Regardless of our circumstances in life, God will never leave us. All may seem hopeless, your life may be filled with despair and there may be no light at the end of the tunnel. In these times, remember that God is all powerful, He is still on the throne and He will be faithful to see you through the "fire", if you will be faithful to Him! Put on the whole armour of God and stand firm against the fiery darts that are being whirled at you from every direction! As you do, the Lord will walk triumphantly with you through the "fires" of your life.

"Finally, my brethren, be strong in the Lord, and in the power of his might. Put on the whole armour of God, that ye may be able to stand against the wiles of the devil. For we wrestle not against flesh and blood, but against principalities, against powers, against the rulers of the darkness of this world, against spiritual wickedness in high places. Wherefore take unto you the whole armour of God, that ye may be able to withstand in the evil day, and having done all, to stand. Stand therefore, having your loins girt about with truth, and having on the breastplate of righteousness; And your feet shod with the preparation of the gospel of peace; Above all, taking the shield of faith, wherewith ye shall be able to quench all the fiery darts of the wicked. And take the helmet of salvation, and the sword of the Spirit, which is the word of God" (Ephesians 6:10-17).

"Ah Lord GOD! behold, thou hast made the heaven and the earth by thy great power and stretched out arm, and there is nothing too hard for thee" (Jeremiah 32:17).

"I will never leave thee, nor forsake thee" (Hebrews 13:5b).

"Wherein ye greatly rejoice, though now for a season, if need be, ye are in heaviness through manifold temptations: That the trial of your faith, being much more precious than of gold that perisheth though it be tried with fire might be found unto praise and honour and glory at the appearing of Jesus Christ" (I Peter 1:6–7).

Dear God, this "fire" is out of my control! I need the whole armour of God to be able to stand against all the fiery darts that are being thrown at me right now! Please give me strength for the battle ahead, be with me, Lord, through this "fire", protect me and empower me, Lord, and work miraculously, for Your honor and glory!

✝ Real Joy is Available for Our Lives

The message at church was about having real joy in our lives. The preacher shared from Philippians chapter 4 how our joy can endure whatever happens in our life, and we can have joy regardless of our circumstances.

Real joy is found in reading God's Word and prayer. Peace *with* God comes at the time we accept Jesus Christ into our lives as our personal Savior and Lord. Peace *of* God comes when we surrender to God's will for our lives!

Are you longing for *real* joy in your life—joy even in the midst of difficult circumstances? Turn to Jesus—He is the Author and Sustainer of our lives and the Source for true joy!

> "Rejoice in the Lord always: and again I say, Rejoice" (Philippians 4:4).

> "Be careful for nothing; but in everything by prayer and supplication with thanksgiving let your requests

be made known unto God. And the peace of God, which passeth all understanding, shall keep your hearts and minds through Christ Jesus" (Philippians 4:6–7).

Dear God, keep me on my knees in prayer and in Your Word each day, for only there will I find true peace, nourishment, and joy for my soul. You know the circumstances in my life right now, Lord. You know the battles that are raging. Comfort me, Lord, strengthen me, Lord, and fill my soul with true joy this day and in the days ahead.

✝ Blessings in the Midst of the Storm

My husband and I attended an informational class at the hospital for those who would be starting chemotherapy treatments. As the nurse explained all the possible challenges that lay ahead, discouragement began to creep into my heart and mind. It was difficult mentally to sit there with several other couples and hear what was ahead for us. *Do I have the strength to make it through what lies ahead?* I wondered. My faith was shaken, and I had to ask the Lord to again get my feet out of the miry clay and to put them back on the solid Rock.

One lighthearted moment at the meeting was when we were told we could eat whatever we felt like eating during the chemotherapy treatments! *Oh, boy—ice cream!* I thought. Of course, I realized we were being challenged to eat whatever or whenever we felt we could during the treatments because our desire for food would change due to nausea and other side effects. But, for just a moment, the Lord brought a little joy to my heart by the fact that I would be able to eat whatever I wanted in the days and months ahead.

Just like the children of Israel experienced God's provision in their time in the wilderness, God continues to take care of His children today in our times of need. May these verses remind us all of God's continued blessings in our lives each day.

> "Yet thou in thy manifold mercies forsookest them not in the wilderness: the pillar of the cloud departed not from them by day, to lead them in the way; neither the pillar of fire by night, to shew them light, and the way wherein they should go. Thou gavest also thy good spirit to instruct them, and withheldest not thy manna from their mouth, and gavest them water for their thirst. Yea, forty years didst thou sustain them in the wilderness, so that they lacked nothing; their clothes waxed not old, and their feet swelled not" (Nehemiah 9:19-21).

Thank you, God, for Your presence in our lives and Your continued blessings in the midst of the storms.

✝ God Even Cares about My Hair

It was time to go shopping for a wig. I had planned to go the week before but didn't have the courage to go. The thought of losing my hair and having to wear a wig was just so distressing.

God was faithful once again, though, and two wonderful ladies were working at the store when I arrived. They were very knowledgeable of their products and sensitive to my situation. They worked with me to find just the right wig for me, which would look very similar to my hair style and color. *Wow,* I thought—*God even cares about my hair and the way I look!*

"Are not two sparrows sold for a farthing? And one of them shall not fall on the ground without your Father. But the very hairs of your head are all numbered. Fear ye not therefore, ye are of more value than many sparrows" (Matthew 10:29–31).

Thank you, God, for creating me and caring about every detail of my life—even my hair and the way I look. Please help me to trust You completely with my life and walk with me through whatever is ahead.

✠ God Guides Us Step by Step

As you can imagine, I dreaded the oncology appointment when the doctor and I were to discuss starting chemotherapy treatments. However, as the doctor entered the room and we began discussing my weekly schedule, God gave me the opportunity and the boldness to share with her that I was a Christian, and Sundays were the most important day of the week to me. I told her I loved going to church and being involved and didn't want to miss Sundays by being sick. I asked her if Monday afternoons would be a possibility for the treatments, and she said yes, Mondays would be a great time.

This experience was just another confirmation in my heart that the Lord was leading and guiding and cares about every detail of my life, even the day of the week that I have chemotherapy treatments! God was so faithful to me once again, and as I saw Him guiding me at every stage of my journey with cancer, His peace again flooded my soul. I was reminded once again that, as His child, I was in His loving care.

"I will instruct thee and teach thee in the way which thou shalt go: I will guide thee with mine eye" (Psalm 32:8).

"Thou wilt keep him in perfect peace, whose mind is stayed on thee: because he trusteth in thee" (Isaiah 26:3).

Thank you, God, that You have a plan for my life and You have orchestrated every detail—even the day I have chemotherapy treatments! What a mighty God we serve!

✝ May Others See Jesus in Me

One morning, one of the staff members in my office came to talk with me, to ask how I was doing. I had learned over the past few months that a question like this one was an opportunity to tell someone about the Lord, so I began to share with him just how good God had been to me and how mightily He had been working in my life.

The co-worker replied that he could see the "old" Barbara and now the "new" Barbara—not that the old me was bad, but that God was doing such a work in my life that he noticed the difference. Praise God!

Can people see Jesus working in your life? Being on this journey with cancer has been extremely difficult, but it's not about me--it's all about how powerful God is and how He can do abundantly above all we could ever ask or think possible, especially in the darkest times of our lives, for His honor and glory!

"Let your light so shine before men, that they may see your good works, and glorify your Father which is in heaven" (Matthew 5:16).

"If any man speak, let him speak as the oracles of God; if any man minister, let him do it as of the ability which God giveth: that God in all things may be glorified through Jesus Christ, to whom be praise and dominion for ever and ever. Amen" (I Peter 4:11).

Dear Jesus, Please continue to shine through me!

✝ Opportunities All Around Us

I went shopping one day during my lunch break, only to learn when I arrived at the store that they were out of the items I needed. Wishing I had gone to a different store, I turned the corner on the aisle to leave and found two ladies talking. One was saying how she was going into the hospital that week for surgery for cancer and was shopping for several things she would need while in the hospital.

A short time later, as we were both leaving the store, I noticed that the lady was ahead of me. I stopped her outside, telling her that I heard her say she was having surgery for cancer. I shared how I had just gone through surgery, was starting chemotherapy soon, and would be praying for her as she had her surgery that week. We talked for a few minutes, and then she thanked me as she went on her way.

This lady was eighty-three years young and the caregiver for her husband. After our conversation, I thanked the Lord for the opportunity to be of encouragement to someone else who was on her own journey with cancer and for the opportunity to pray for her in the days ahead.

> "Blessed be God, even the Father of our Lord Jesus Christ, the Father of mercies, and the God of all comfort; Who comforteth us in all our tribulation, that we may be able to comfort them which are in any trouble, by the comfort wherewith we ourselves are comforted of God" (2 Corinthians 1:3–4).

Thank you, God, for leading me to and through every situation I encounter, even when I think the situation is for naught. You may always have a dear soul in that place who needs some encouragement. Thank you for giving me ears to hear others' needs and the opportunity to speak words to them in Jesus' name. Open my eyes and my heart to other opportunities You have for me to encourage someone else who is on a road with cancer, just like me.

✞ A Light in a Dark Place

On the morning that my chemotherapy treatments began, the Lord directed me to these verses in the Bible, reminding me that my thoughts should not be on my circumstances but on Him and the opportunity He placed before me to bring some light, His light, into a dark place—to share Christ with a world searching for lasting hope.

On that day, I wrote these words:

I am going into the unknown today, and my flesh is scared, but I know the Lord is with me, and He will not leave me or forsake me. God will walk with me through this deep, dark valley today.

> "Ye are the light of the world. A city that is set on a hill cannot be hid. Neither do men light a candle, and put it under a bushel, but on a candlestick; and it giveth light unto all that are in the house" (Matthew 5:14–15).

According to these verses, a single candle can make a *huge* difference in a dark place.

Lord, I'm just one person, but I'm created in Your image for Your glory. As I walk through the unknown today, please let Your light shine through me in a dark place to all that are in the room.

✟ Another Opportunity— The Umbrella Story

I had started losing my hair from the chemotherapy treatments, so I went to the mall to purchase the wig I had selected several weeks earlier. I made my purchase and was on my way out of the mall when I noticed the pouring rain—so I went back into the store to buy an umbrella.

That's when the Lord sent Alfred to assist me with my purchase. He showed me the selection of umbrellas they had in stock, and after making my selection, I opened one umbrella to make sure it worked properly. Alfred quickly commented about the superstition of bad luck and opened umbrellas indoors.

This comment gave me the opportunity that I needed to share with Alfred about the Lord, so I replied that I didn't believe in luck, but that I believed in God. I told Alfred that God was my best friend, and that He had been with me every step of the way the past few months as I went through surgery for cancer and now chemotherapy. He was so surprised and said I didn't look like someone that had cancer, because—I was so happy. I asked Alfred if He knew the Lord and had a personal relationship with Him. His answer was that he had gone to church, been in the choir, and so forth, but that church just didn't work for him. As we talked further, it was obvious that Alfred was searching for a true, personal relationship with God.

Do you know Jesus in a personal way? Jesus is standing at the door of your heart, and He wants to come in and have fellowship with you. Will you open the door and let Him in?

> "Behold, I stand at the door, and knock: if any man hear my voice, and open the door, I will come in to him, and will sup with him, and he with me" (Revelation 3:20).

Dear Jesus, Thank you for loving me, for dying on the cross for my sin. Please come into my heart now, Lord Jesus, forgive me of all my sin, and give me true peace and rest in my soul. I need You, Lord.

✟ Changes and Transition

As the chemotherapy treatments progressed, the time came when I began to lose my hair. After several days of this gradual transition, the day came when the hair that remained would be gone too. Unaware of what was about to happen, I went to take a shower on that Saturday morning. It was then that I realized this was "the day" I had prepared for, but I was not ready for it when it came! Suddenly my hair was falling out in my hands! With tears streaming down my face and my hair flowing into my hands, I found myself totally broken emotionally.

It was in that moment of despair, that God revealed His presence to me once again. For out of the depths of my soul, I began to worship the Lord by singing the Doxology to Him: *Praise God, from whom all blessings flow; Praise Him, all creatures here below; Praise Him above, ye heav'nly host; Praise Father, Son, and Holy Ghost.*

My flesh could not sing these words—my heart was *broken.* Yet in my brokenness, God was there, and my soul praised Him for who He is—a great and mighty, true and living God, Creator of my life. As my heart was breaking, my soul could still trust in the Lord and sing praises to Him, even in the midst of the storm.

Thank you, God, for hearing the cries of Your children, for allowing us to know You are with us in our times of deepest need, and for giving us the ability to continue to praise You through difficult times! What a mighty God You are!

"I cried unto the LORD with my voice, and he heard me out of his holy hill. Selah" (Psalm 3:4).

✟ Internal Beauty

I had lost all my hair, which took me a while to adjust to—the look of my bald head in the mirror each morning was a very difficult thing to see and a difficult transition to make.

As I sought the Lord for strength, He reminded me from His Word that what was important was not the outward woman that others see, but the internal being. Our bodies change and are corruptible, but the internal is incorruptible.

At this time in my life, my flesh was corruptible—I had had surgery for cancer, and now my body was changed and had scars which I would have for the rest of my life. I had no hair, and I was going through chemotherapy treatments which were killing cells all throughout my body.

Our physical bodies are always changing. Our circumstances always change. There is never a time, however, that God is not with us, regardless of what changes we go through in life. God never changes. He is the same yesterday, today, and forever.

> "Whose adorning let it not be that outward adorning of plaiting the hair (I had no hair left to plait!), and of wearing of gold, or of putting on of apparel; But let it be the hidden man of the heart, in that which is not corruptible, even the ornament of a meek and quiet spirit, which is in the sight of God of great price" (1 Peter 3:3–4).

Thank you, Lord, for Your encouragement and for reminding me that my hair is not what is important, but it is the internal beauty that You are working on in me. Lord, please let Your beauty shine through me.

✝ Everyday Blessings

On my mother's 75th birthday, I realized how very blessed I have been all these years to have such a wonderful mother, one who has prayed for me and been a godly example to me through her life each day. Mom has such a giving heart and finds joy in serving others. She is also a cancer survivor and uses this experience in her life to encourage others in their journey with cancer.

Praise God from whom all blessings flow...Thank you, Lord, for your little, every day blessings that we so often take for granted:

- *Thank you that I can now get out of the bed in the morning without hurting.*

- *Thank you that I can walk through the house without internally feeling every step.*

- *Thank you that I can now bend over without hurting—I can bend over and put dirty dishes in the dishwasher again or bend over to take clothes out of the washer and put them in the dryer.*

- *Thank you that I can now sit down again without hurting or lay on my side again without hurting.*

- *Thank you for strength to be able to walk through the grocery store and push a grocery cart again.*

- *Thank you for the strength to be able to stand in the kitchen and cook meals for my family.*

- *Thank you, Lord, for strength to do everyday things again, which we so often take for granted and sometimes complain about having to do.*

Now these everyday tasks are blessings to me, things that I once took for granted; now I am grateful for the strength to be able to do them again for my family.

Even though I was in the middle of chemotherapy treatments and had lost all my hair, I praised the Lord for His goodness to me these past few months and for His faithfulness to me, guiding me day by day, step by step, and taking care of me all the way.

"I will sing of the mercies of the LORD for ever: with my mouth will I make known thy faithfulness to all generations." (Psalm 89:1).

"O give thanks unto the LORD; for he is good: because his mercy endureth for ever" (Psalm 118:1).

Thank you, God, for Your loving care.

✝ God Can Even Use My Wig!

One morning in the midst of chemotherapy treatments, I went to my son's cross country race. Hundreds of people were there, and amongst all the activity of the race, God was working. He allowed me to share with two ladies about what He was doing in my life. I had not seen either of these ladies for a while, and neither of them knew what had been happening in my life. I was able to share with them of God's faithfulness to me through the cancer, surgery, and now chemotherapy treatments. The Lord even used my "new hair" to bring one of them over to me. She said she had been wondering all morning who I was and didn't recognize me because of my new "hairstyle." She was actually looking for a new style for her hair and wanted to compliment me on mine.

The Lord used this opportunity for me to share with these ladies about God's working in my life. *Wow,* I thought, *God can even use my wig to open doors of opportunity to share with others about Him!* Praise the Lord! God is continuing to touch lives!

"Wherefore seeing we also are compassed about with so great a cloud of witnesses, let us lay aside every weight, and the sin which doth so easily beset us, and let us run with patience the race that is set before us. Looking unto Jesus the author and finisher of our faith; who for the joy that was set before him endured the cross, despising the shame, and is set down at the right hand of the throne of God" (Hebrews 12:1-2).

"Let your light so shine before men, that they may see your good works, and glorify your Father which is in heaven" (Matthew 5:16).

Oh, God, here I am in the middle of chemotherapy treatments, I'm weak, and I've lost all of my hair, but You are still able to use me to accomplish Your will. Thank you, God, for this opportunity. Please continue to strengthen me and help me to see the opportunities You have prepared all around me. May I let Your light continue to shine through me each day.

✝ Mental Challenges

As I awoke one particular morning, I found my mind struggling with the thought of another treatment. My eyes were focused on my physical situation and the expected side effects, rather than on what the Lord wanted to do in and through me that day.

Then the time came for my next treatment, and to my surprise, while the nurse administered the chemotherapy drugs to me, I had the opportunity to share with her all about how God was working in my life—what a captive audience!

Even when we feel weak and inadequate, God still wants to work through us. It is through our weakness that He is made strong.

> "Thou wilt keep him in perfect peace, whose mind is stayed on thee: because he trusteth in thee. Trust ye in the LORD for ever: for in the LORD JEHOVAH is everlasting strength" (Isaiah 26:3–4).

"And the peace of God, which passeth all understanding, shall keep your hearts and minds through Christ Jesus" (Philippians 4:7).

Thank you, Lord, for another opportunity to share with others what You are doing in my life. Thank you for helping me to get my mind off of myself and my current situation and turning my focus to someone that needs to hear about You.

✝ I Need You, Lord!

The weeks became long as the side effects grew stronger with each treatment. My mind struggled as well as my flesh. I needed the Lord's strength.

The Lord brought these verses to my mind:

> "He gives power to the weak, And to those who have no might He increases strength" (Isaiah 40:29).

> "I can do all things through Christ which strengtheneth me" (Philippians 4:13).

Lord, I feel so weak and don't know how I am going to make it through the rest of the treatments. Please help me to keep my mind on You, to remember that You won't ask me to go through anything alone, that You are with me and will give me strength for each new day! Please help me to stay focused on Your plan for my life and to remember that I am in Your hands. I need You, Lord!

✝ God's Grace Is Sufficient

In 2 Corinthians chapter 11, we are reminded of all the Apostle Paul suffered. Among many things, he was shipwrecked out at sea, hungry and thirsty, imprisoned, beaten and stoned multiple times, and as if these trials weren't enough, he had a "thorn in the flesh," which he asked the Lord three times to remove.

Verse 9 tells of how the Lord responds to the Apostle Paul's request, "My grace is sufficient for thee: for my strength is made perfect in weakness." The Lord didn't remove Paul's "thorn in the flesh," but He was with Paul, and He will be with us in our time of need as well. It is so true that when we are at our weakest, His strength is truly revealed. Rest in God's grace, and let it be sufficient for you!

> "For this thing I besought the Lord thrice, that it might depart from me. And he said unto me, My grace is sufficient for thee: for my strength is made perfect in weakness. Most gladly therefore will I rather glory in my infirmities, that the power of Christ may rest upon me" (2 Corinthians 12:8-9).

✝ Cherish the Day

On the way home from my son's cross-country race, I saw a tag on a car that said "Cherish the Day." How true that statement is! Each day is now so much sweeter and so much more precious than before my diagnosis with cancer, that I don't want to waste a single one. Days that I used to take for granted or complain about are now God-given gifts to me!

I used to want to hear the Lord say to me at the end of my life, "Well done, good and faithful servant"—but not anymore. Now I have a daily perspective. At the end of *each day,* when I put my head on my pillow at night and ask the Lord if He was pleased with me that day, I want to hear Him say, *Yes; well done, good and faithful servant.*

This day-by-day mentality has changed my whole perspective on life. Each individual day and the opportunities before me now hold more value. Remember—none of us are guaranteed tomorrow. We only have today, *right now.*

"Whereas ye know not what shall be on the morrow. For what is your life? It is even a vapor, that appeareth for a little time, and then vanisheth away" (James 4:14).

"Boast not thyself of tomorrow; for thou knowest not what a day may bring forth" (Proverbs 27:1).

"This is the day which the LORD hath made; we will rejoice and be glad in it" (Psalm 118:24).

God is the giver and the sustainer of life. Our time here on the earth is so short, like a vapor that quickly vanishes. On our death beds, what will be important will be what we did for God with our lives. What are you investing *your* life in?

Thank you, Lord, for each new day and the opportunities you have in it, if only I will stop long enough to ask You to guide me and show me Your workings and Your blessings.

✝ More of You, Lord

I received a card in the mail from a lady which read, "I know you have difficult days, but people are seeing Jesus in you." Oh, God, this is my desire—I want them to see You, not me. You are everything, and You are the One to be praised! May this be my daily prayer, for people to see Jesus working in me!

> "Now faith is the substance of things hoped for, the evidence of things not seen. By faith Enoch was translated that he should not see death; and was not found, because God had translated him: for before his translation he had this testimony, that he pleased God" (Hebrews 11:1,5).

> "He must increase, but I must decrease" (John 3:30).

Lord, may my testimony be that I pleased You. May others see You in me!

✝ The Anchor Holds

During another difficult week with chemotherapy treatment, I cried in my husband's arms. As we stood in the kitchen embracing each other, he reminded me of his unfailing love for me and that regardless of our circumstances, if God is for us, who can be against us?

"The LORD is my light and my salvation; whom shall I fear? The LORD is the strength of my life; of whom shall I be afraid? (Psalm 27:1).

"The Lord will give strength unto his people; the Lord will bless his people with peace" (Psalm 29:11).

"He giveth power to the faint; and to them that have no might he increaseth strength" (Isaiah 40:29).

Thank you, God, for my loving husband and for being with me even in my weakness. Please give me strength to carry on!

✝ A Brand New Day

It was the end of another chemotherapy week, and as I awoke one morning, I took a deep breath and thanked the Lord for the new day—a new day without the smell of drugs saturating my body, a new day full of life and opportunities to serve the Lord!

"He brought me up also out of an horrible pit, out of the miry clay, and set my feet upon a rock, and established my goings" (Psalm 40:2).

"This is the day which the LORD hath made; we will rejoice and be glad in it" (Psalm 118:24).

Thank you, Lord, for walking with me through this deep valley and for bringing me out on the other side. Thank you for being victorious in my life once again, and for giving me new life this day! Fill me, Lord, with Your Spirit, and may others see You in me today.

✟ New Beginnings

As I have continued on this journey, God has been speaking to my heart about a new ministry to those whose lives have been touched by cancer—a ministry that would share the gospel message of Jesus Christ and encourage those who are walking down the same path that I have now traveled. As I prayed regarding the Lord's will, God gave me the name for this new ministry: "Courage Through Cancer Ministries." *Thank you, God—how perfect!* I prayed. Going through cancer takes *so* much courage—more courage than I ever thought I had!

I see a great need for such a ministry, not just in my city but also around the world. I can vision this ministry reaching around the globe, as we share the message of true hope in Christ and the "care" of the Lord Jesus with others as they walk down this difficult path—a ministry that would challenge people to live victoriously through cancer and be a shining light for Christ in the process!

"Have not I commanded thee? Be strong and of a good courage; be not afraid, neither be thou dismayed: for the LORD thy God is with thee whithersoever thou goest" (Joshua 1:9).

Thank you, Lord, that You have a purpose for this journey! Give me the courage to follow You, wherever this path may lead.

✟ Start of Public Ministry

The Lord has continued to take me to new levels in my walk with Him and had now presented me with an opportunity to give a testimony at an upcoming ladies' fellowship. Although I appreciated the invitation, I withdrew to my old self and was not ready to commit to giving a public testimony. After all, I have never spoken in front of a crowd and was afraid! The Lord brought me a long way in recent months, changing me from being a private person to now being able to share one-on-one with others about His working in my life, but speaking in front of a group of people was a different story.

I had been pondering this opportunity since it was presented to me several weeks earlier. When I received a phone call about another lady who had been diagnosed with cancer and was facing surgery, I knew it was time to take the next step of faith by publically sharing my testimony. I called the lady who had presented the opportunity to me, and we scheduled a time for me to testify at the ladies' fellowship. This opportunity would allow me to take what the Lord had been teaching me and share it with others; it would be my first public testimony.

Each of us is unique, and each of us has a testimony. Are you allowing the Lord to use you by sharing yours with others?

"I will greatly praise the LORD with my mouth; yea, I will praise him among the multitude" (Psalm 109:30).

"And he hath put a new song in my mouth, even praise unto our God: many shall see it, and fear, and shall trust in the LORD" (Psalm 40:3).

Empower me, Lord, and speak through me for Your glory!

The Joy of the Lord Is My Strength

After my final chemotherapy treatment and a week in bed, I wanted to go to church, because two of my doctors had said they would be there. Still feeling weak, I went anyway, and God had such a blessing in store for me! The message was about Jesus walking on the water from John chapter 5. The pastor told the congregation that regardless of the circumstances in our lives, Jesus can still walk on water, meeting our needs—so we don't have to be afraid!

As I listened to the sermon, I saw one of my doctors sitting in the congregation! Here was someone that I had met as a result of having cancer, and she and her fiancé came to church that day! The joy of the Lord flooded my soul, and I was strengthened physically and spiritually!

"The joy of the Lord is your strength" (Nehemiah 8:10).

Thank you, God, for using me! Even in my weakness, You have been made strong!

✟ A Changed Life!

A week after my last chemotherapy treatment, I found that gradually, my strength was returning, and I began to feel the joy of being finished with that part of my journey with cancer. This week was also the week before Thanksgiving. *This year,* I thought, *will be special as our family rejoices in God's faithfulness to us this year.*

As I close out this book, God has brought me full circle from being a person who could not and would not share with anyone what was happening in my life to being someone who looks for opportunities to tell people everywhere what God has done in my life! My heart truly rejoices in God's mercy and grace to me through the valley of cancer. My soul cannot be silent; I must share with others what God has done in my life and what He will do in and through theirs, too. I would not wish cancer on anyone, but if I had the last year of my life (since my diagnosis) to live over again, I wouldn't change one thing. God has been so real to me; He has walked beside me every step of the way each day, and He has changed my life!

"Thou hast turned for me my mourning unto dancing: thou has put off my sackcloth, and girded me with gladness; To the end that my glory (soul) may sing praise to thee, and not be silent. O LORD my God, I will give thanks unto thee forever" (Psalm 30:11–12).

"I waited patiently for the Lord; and he inclined unto me, and heard my cry. He brought me up also out of a horrible pit, out of the miry clay, and set my feet upon a rock, and established my goings. And he hath put a new song in my mouth, even praise unto our God: many shall see it, and fear, and shall trust in the Lord" (Psalm 40:1–3).

✝ Do You Know Him?

Are you burdened by the path you are on today and in need of some peace and rest? Would you like to know for sure that you are going to heaven at the end of your life?

Jesus said,

> "I am come that they might have life, and that they might have it more abundantly" (John 10:10b).

> "I am the way, the truth, and the life: no man cometh unto the Father, but by me" (John 14:6).

> "Come unto me, all ye that labour and are heavy laden, and I will give you rest" (Matthew 11:28).

> "Casting all your care upon him; for he careth for you" (I Peter 5:7).

> "Draw nigh to God, and He will draw nigh to you" (James 4:8).

"Look unto me, and be ye saved, all the ends of the earth: for I am God, and there is none else" (Isaiah 45:22).

"When Jesus heard it, he saith unto them, They that are whole have no need of the physician, but they that are sick: I came not to call the righteous, but sinners to repentance" (Mark 2:17).

"For the wages of sin is death; but the gift of God is eternal life through Jesus Christ our Lord" (Romans 6:23).

"For God so loved the world, that he gave his only begotten Son, that whosoever believed in him should not perish, but have everlasting life" (John 3:16).

The Bible teaches us how to have peace and rest, life more abundantly, and eternal life in heaven.

1. Repent of your sins. "For all have sinned and come short of the glory of God" Romans 3:23. "Except ye repent, ye shall all likewise perish" Luke 13:3.

2. Believe the Gospel: Jesus is the Son of God, Jesus died on the cross for our sins, God raised Jesus back to life bodily, and He is alive today and is coming back to earth again.

3. By faith, receive Jesus Christ into your heart and life as Savior and Lord by praying this prayer with your mouth and believing it in your heart: *Dear Jesus, I need You in my life. I cannot go through this without You. I know*

that You love me. Please come into my heart, forgive me of my sins, and be my Savior and Lord. Walk with me all the rest of my life, and take me to heaven when I die. In Jesus name I pray, Amen.

If you prayed that prayer just now and meant it in your heart, then God heard you, and you are now His child. Rest in His arms, lean on Him, and let Him walk with you through the storms of life—even a life with cancer!

Jesus said,

> "That if thou shalt confess with thy mouth the Lord Jesus, and shalt believe in thine heart that God hath raised him from the dead, thou shalt be saved" (Romans 10:9).

> "And I give unto them eternal life; and they shall never perish, neither shall any man pluck them out of my hand" (John 10:28).

God will walk with you in the darkest times of your life, and He will be there at the end of your life and forever after. He will never leave you nor forsake you, regardless of what comes into your life. Just trust Him!

> "Trust in him at all times; ye people, pour out your heart before him: God is a refuge for us. Selah." (Psalm 62:8).

May the Lord bless you and may His light shine through you.

Courage Through Cancer Ministries, Inc.

PO Box 4067, Tallahassee, FL 32315-4067

Cancer Care Line: 1-855-6-COURAGE

CourageThroughCancer.com